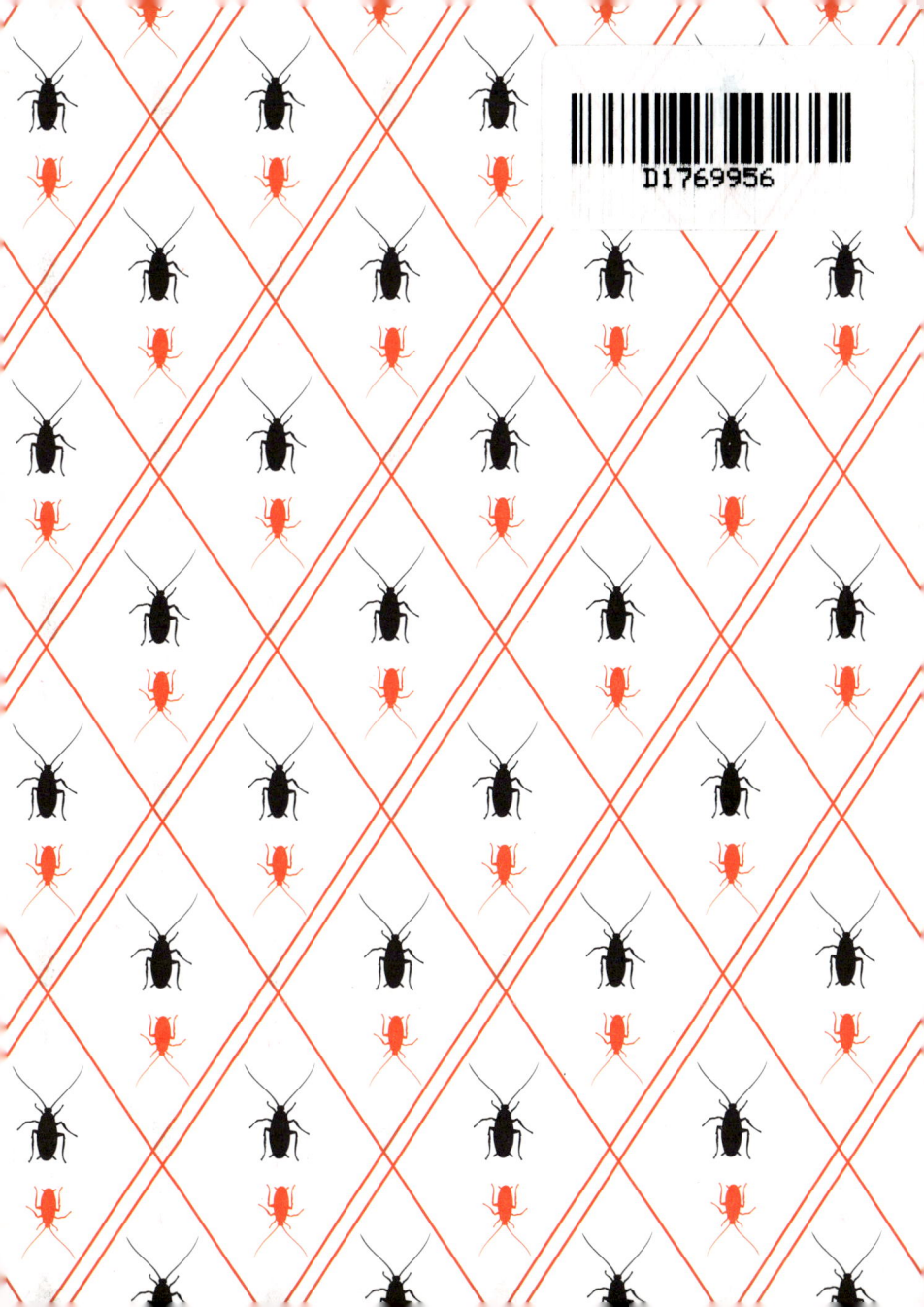

an illustrated guide to

Cock-
roaches

BY EKATERINA SMIRNOVA

mbp

Contents

Word from the author   **6**

Introduction

Chapter I
THE USUAL SUSPECTS   **10**

American
German
Asian
Size matters
Anatomical system
Different languages
How did that happen?
Roach babies
A little albino
Your housemate
Darkness
Family tree
Worldwide

Chapter II
ROACH TALENTS   **38**

How fast?
Pushing the limit
Head off
Peek-a-boo

Chapter III
DINING ETIQUETTE

Medicine
Disease
Delicacy

Chapter IV
TO BE OR NOT TO BE?

Pest control
Vegas roach trap
Labyrinth

Chapter V
ROACH INTELLIGENCE

Morning incompetence
Roach democracy
Smugglers

Chapter VI
ROACH SCIENCE FICTION

Zombie
Robot 4 roach
Per aspera ad astra
Double cross

Chapter VII
NOT THE BEETLES – THE ROACHES

Pop culture
Roach dream dictionary

HAPPY END

Acknowledgements

Word from the author

Please, please don't consider me crazy. I don't have any special obsession with 🪳s. As a matter of fact I am not even friends with them, check on my Facebook page if you don't believe me. They are one of the few insects of which I have always been afraid. Every time I meet 🪳s face to face I cannot stop myself from screaming, which probably pleases them and makes them think, "That's right, that's the kind of respect I expect from you, human" (if their thinking was that advanced).

This book is an experiment, a study of the power of graphic design. It all started in the editorial design class of Genevieve Williams at the School of Visual Arts. I had to come up with an idea for a book and then illustrate it. It seemed boring to just make an illustration and a layout for an existing book. So, after brainstorming with my husband, Brian Schmitz, at a New York cafe, we came up with a great idea: I could find the most tedious subject possible and turn it into something that would be interesting to read and study! 🪳s were it! They are more than tedious, they are absolutely disgusting. People don't even want to think about them, let alone read a book about them. Excellent!

Now, how do I possibly make readers want to look at this book? That is challenging, no? Well, my theory was simple: make it fun and visually catchy. And there I was, studying with a magnifying glass a half-eaten 🪳 found in the basement of my apartment, storing pictures on my hard drive, translating articles from my native language Russian to English and back, experimenting with 🪳 traps… Ah, the most fun was to observe differences in a pregnant 🪳 with an egg and one without, up close… while I was eating pasta fagioli soup.

Now see for yourself if I did a good job. I based this book on facts about 🪳s. Please do not judge me too harshly if you find mistakes, I am still an amateur entomologist.

— *Ekaterina Smirnova*

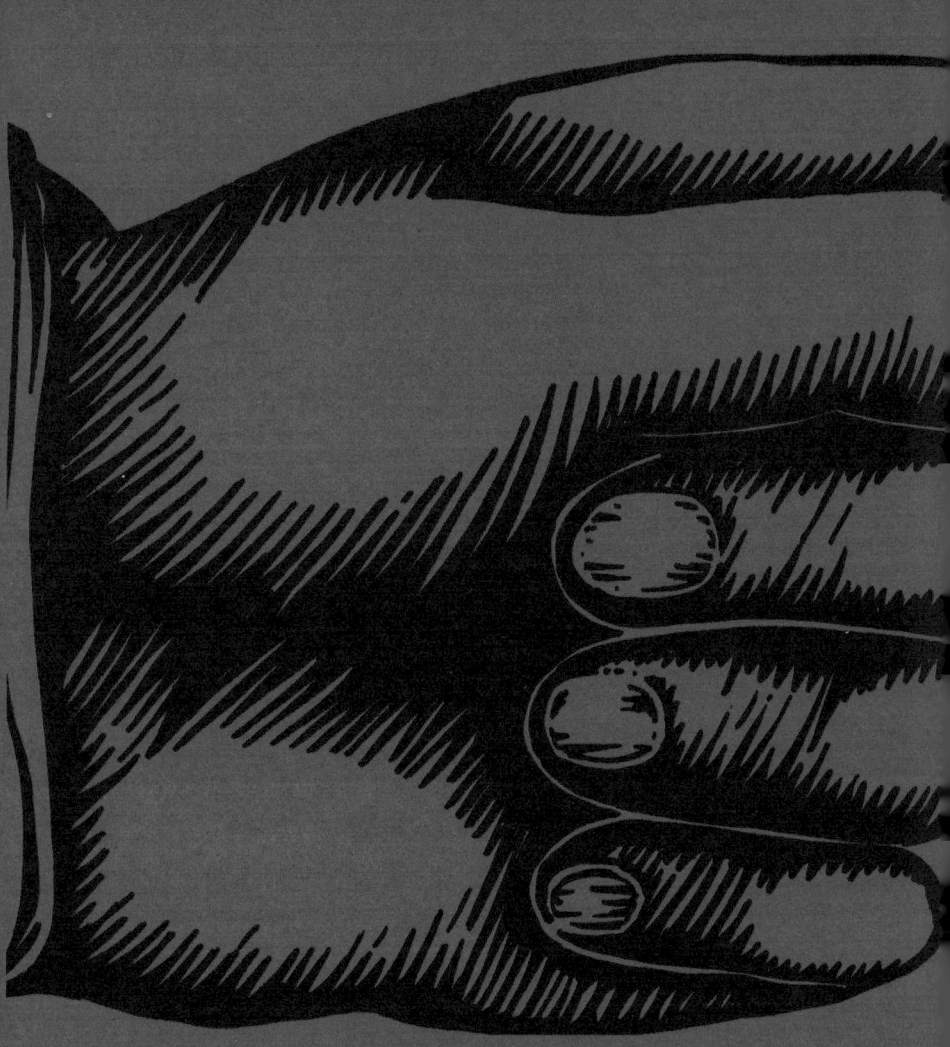

Look at this handsome gentleman with his impressive mustache! What charisma! He is from the noble family of German Cockroaches, a family with a 350-million-year history; he has earned the attention of all humans living on Earth; people know his face. His heritage is filled with trials and tribulations—Ice Ages, atomic tests, pest control—but nothing has been

able to break the incredible will of our hero. Because of their remarkable reproductive system and adaptability to the environment and to poisons, cockroaches continue to live and to please the inhabitants of our planet.

Allow me to present, Mr. Cockroach! Please treat him with love and care.

CHAPTER I

The Usual Suspects

MEET THE FAMILY

american

The American cockroach

Common characteristics: The American cockroach (Latin: *Periplaneta americana*) is the largest member of the cockroach family. It mainly inhabits the Americas, hence the name.

Employment type: De-sanitization of restaurants, bakeries, breweries, pet shops, and other establishments that contain or produce food.

Habitats: In your house, under your house, in your sewage system, in your basement.

Preferred mode of transportation: In boxes or luggage sent from the North American continent.

Diet: Never diets. He eats almost everything, leaving marks and smells on books, wallpaper, and floor tiles.

Special abilities: Fastest insect in the world; can reach speeds of up to 37 miles per hour (60 km per hour). He is very hard to catch when discovered committing a crime. Adults may even take to flight for escape. (Young cockroaches resemble adults, but their wings haven't developed yet.)

Color: Reddish-brown with yellow spots on the back.

Size: Adult beetles reach up to 2.5 inches (6.5 cm) in length, not counting their huge antennae.

The German cockroach

Common characteristics: German cockroach (Latin: *Blattella germanica*). Undoubtedly a guest in every house (they are synanthropic, i.e. he lives wherever humans do). He is the fourth most common house pest, and also the most common of the cockroaches.

Employment Type: Unemployed. Unabashedly lives off the generosity of man.

Habitats: Lives in a large family in all corners and crevices of your home. He likes warm environments: low temperatures (23 F/-5 C) are lethal to him. In cold climates he can only live in well-heated homes.

Preferred mode of transportation: Stowing away in old boxes, furniture, and bags of vegetables. These roaches will move from building to building during the warm summer months.

Diet: What have you got?

Special abilities: Top-notch survival skills.

Color: Adults are light brown except for two dark brown longitudinal stripes on the back. The young cockroach has wings and is almost black with a light stripe on the back.

Size: Adults reach 0.6 inches (1.5 cm) in length, not counting the antennae.

GeRmAn

asIan

The Asian cockroach

Common characteristics: (Latin: *Blattella asahinai*), the Asian cockroach. Almost identical to the German cockroach except that its wings are longer.

Habitats: Prefers outdoor living in Japan, but is also found in tropical and subtropical climates of the US.

Preferred mode of transportation: Self-propelled flight. Strong wings are a major asset for Asian cockroaches.

Diet: Under certain conditions, feeds on the eggs of other pests.

Specification: Strongly attracted to light. Flies to light-colored and illuminated surfaces; be advised to keep the window screens on while watching television.

Color: Asian cockroaches are slightly lighter in color than German cockroaches.

Size: Adults reach 0.6 inches (1.6 cm) in length, not counting the antennae.

1.0–1.4 cm

German cockroach
Blattella germanica

1.8–2.3 cm

Surinam cockroach
Pycnoscelus surinamensis

2–3 cm

Common methana cockroach
Methana marginalis

Colossus cockroach
Megaloblatta longipennis

8–9.5 cm

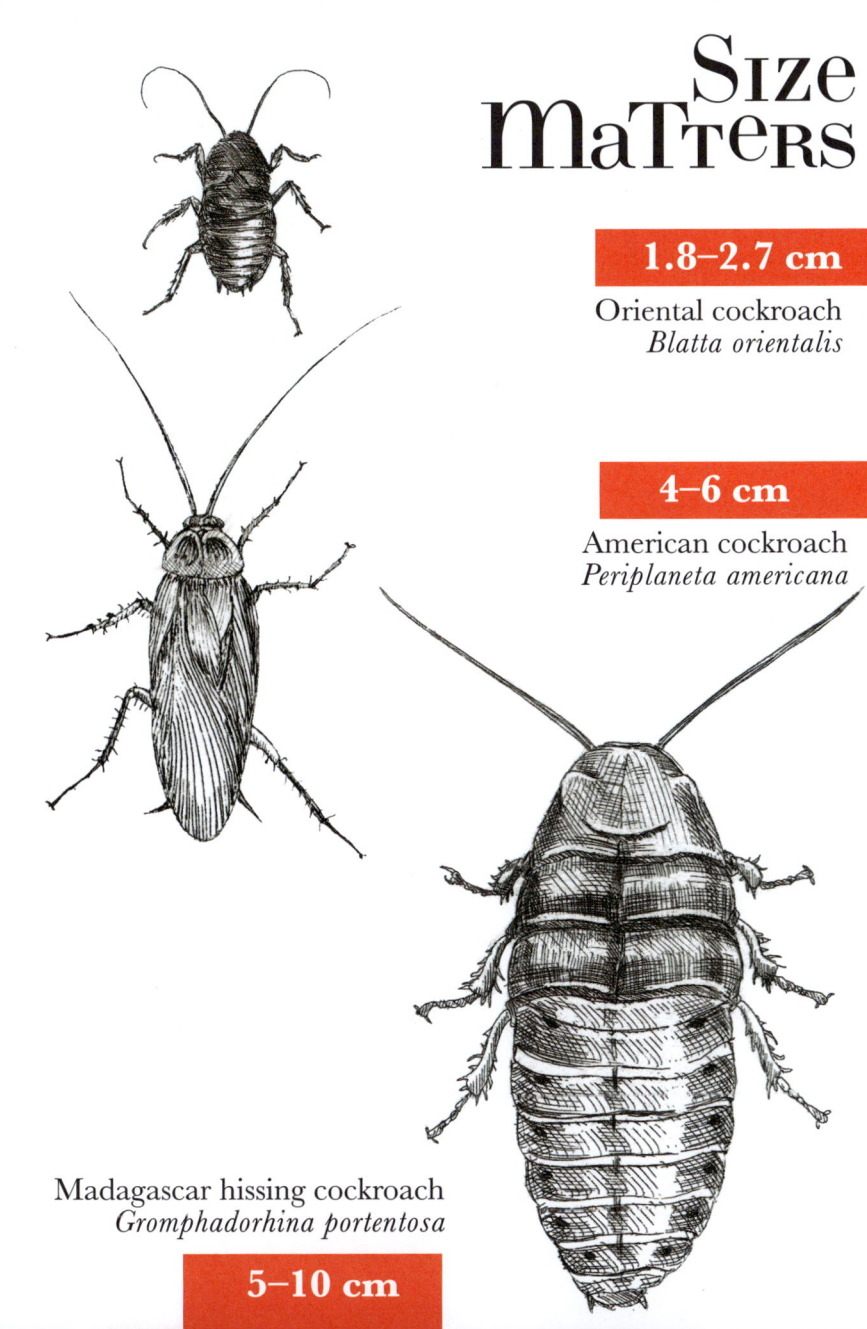

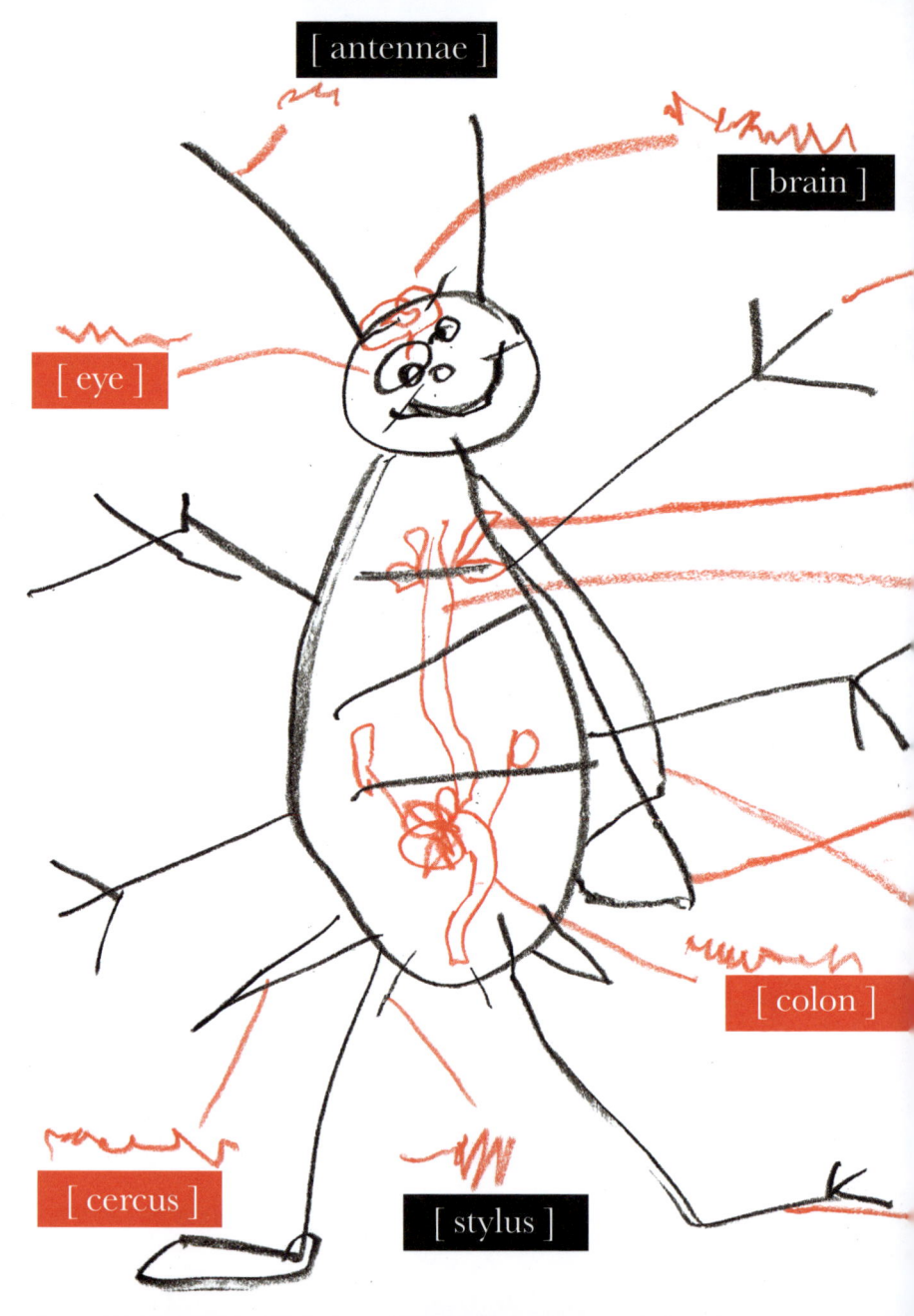

anatomical System

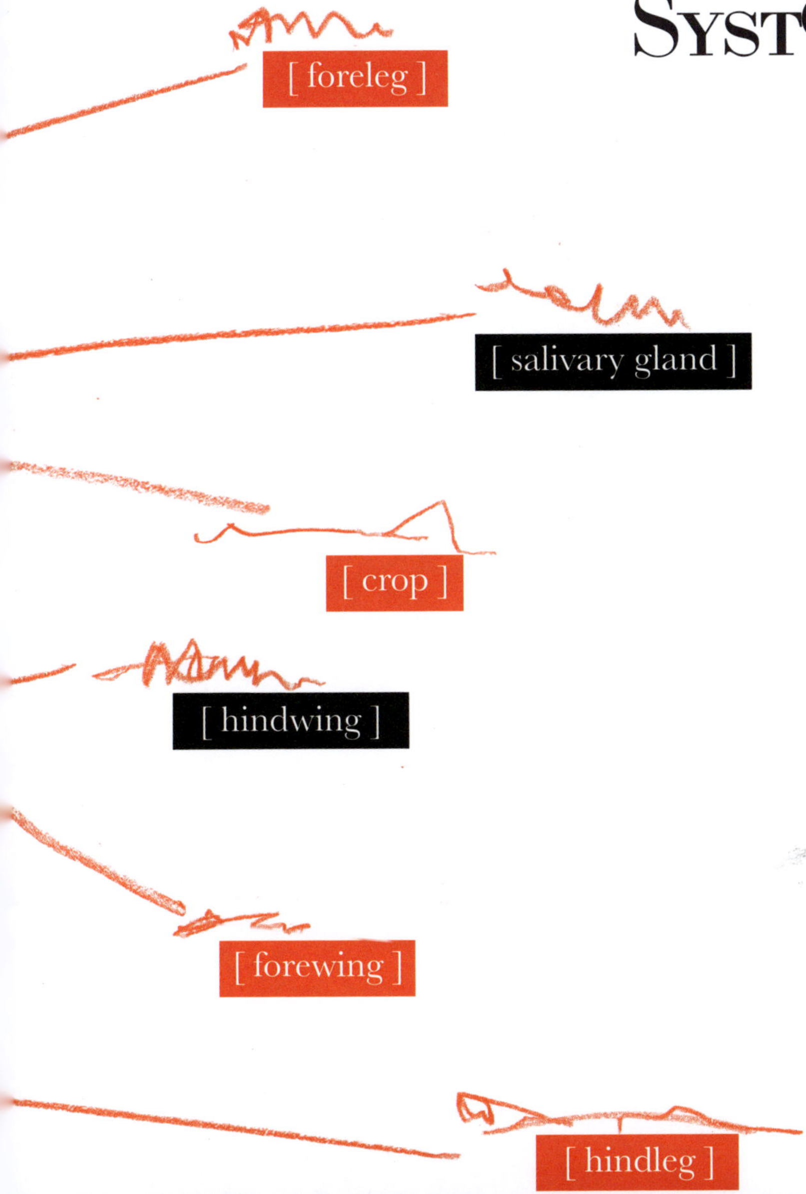

[foreleg]

[salivary gland]

[crop]

[hindwing]

[forewing]

[hindleg]

Dansk (Danish) - ka
(Dutch) - **kakkerla**
- **cafard**; Deutsch (
Küchenschabe ;
- **κατσαρίδα**; 日本
ゴキブリ;Português (
(f) (Zool.); Русский
Español (Spanish) -
(Swedish) - **kackerl**
(Simplified) - 蟑;
퀴벌레, 소기업가,
바쁜 사람; תירבע
Italiano (Italian)
العربية (Arabic) -

kerlak; Nederlands; Français (French) (German) - Kakerlak, Ελληνική (Greek) 語 (Japanese) - Portuguese) - barata (Russian) - таракан; cucaracha; Svenska cka; 中文 (Chinese) - 국어 (Korean) - 바자잘한 일로 몹시 (Hebrew) - קקמ, וקית; - scarafaggio; صرا ص; صرصور (مسال

Imagine a fine morning. A lady cockroach, all dressed up and wearing her special perfume, goes hunting. Like many overly scented women, she's looking for a man. Her perfume works amazingly well, attracting male roaches from all over town. Overwhelmed by the competition, the boys organize a tournament in honor of the fragrant beauty. The conqueror of her heart is the strongest roach of all, making him more… *successful* than the others.

How did that happen?

Later, the young couple leave for more private quarters and…

he

she   her

then

and again

and one more time

again

after

CENSORED

… finally the satisfied male departs, leaving behind a fertilized female. Now she is on her own.

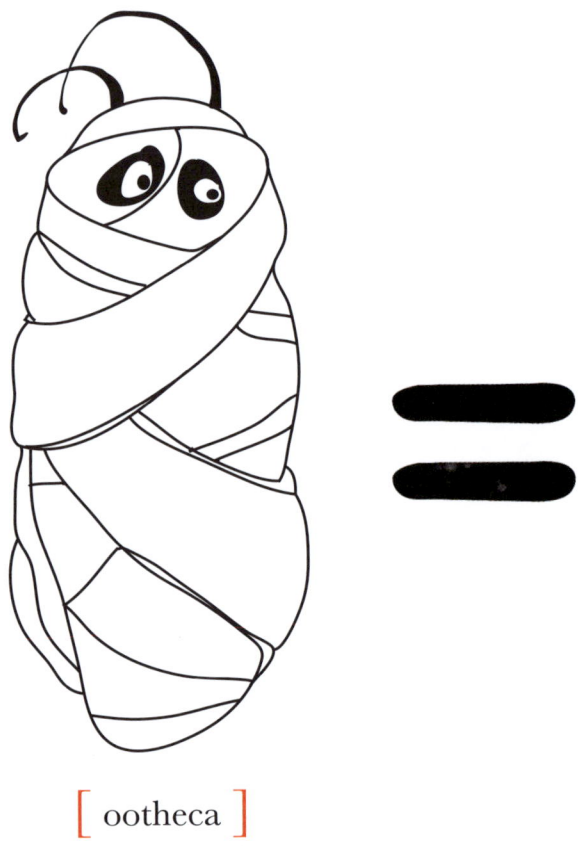

[ootheca]

After a several weeks (two to seven, depending on the type of cockroach) the female will be ready to part with her eggs. She's been carrying them in a special bag called an ootheca. The number of eggs in an ootheca varies by species. This bag is a safe place in a chaotic world,

Roach Babies

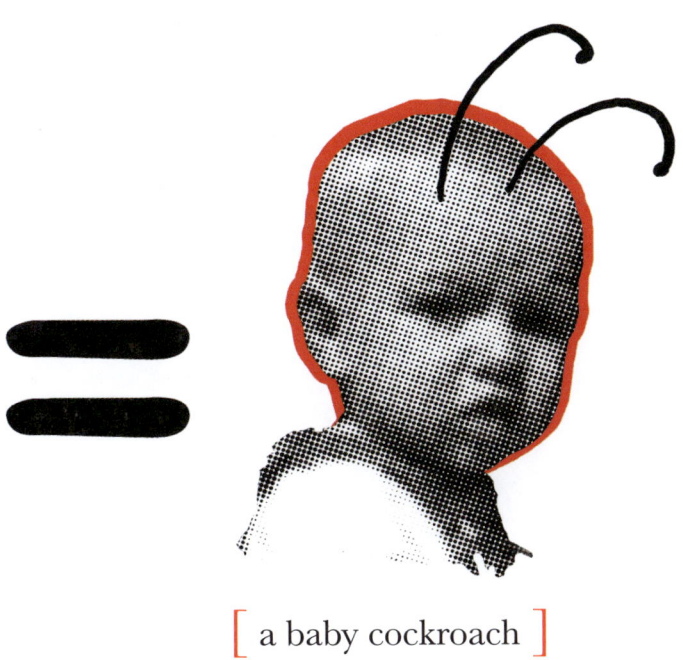

[a baby cockroach]

withstanding cold weather and even pesticides. Many females shed or hide their ootheca before the eggs are ready to hatch, while others continue to carry hatched eggs for a long time. But every type of roach must keep their eggs moist, so that the mustached kids can develop.

Creamy white from top to bottom, a baby cockroach stands out in family pictures. His brand new skin (cuticle) hasn't yet hardened and darkened, making the young albino very vulnerable to any predators who are lucky enough to find him. The soft, creamy white skin is so tender and tasty! Luckily for him it only takes a few hours to mature and transform his pale, soft skin to strong, brown armor. He's a spitting image of his dad after all!

[hard cuticle cockroach]
a few hours after
losing its shell

a little albino

[soft cuticle cockroach
newly molted]

In apartment 1A—as well as in apartments 1B to 20G—a redheaded, mustachioed neighbor appears to have taken up residence. Have you noticed? Whether or not you have, in fact he and his family have always lived there. Many cockroaches are dependent on human activities; that's why they are such frequent guests in your home.

Cockroach Nation is a significant part of the global food system. These omnivorous hunters help clean the environment by eating and processing just about every kind of organic waste. Among the more than 3,000 species of cockroaches, only ten species are on the World Health Organization's list of human pests. All other roaches live outdoors.

People fear cockroaches in part because they are carriers of bacteria that, when in contact with food, increases the risk of asthma and allergic reactions.

and thus IT IS BETTER →

YOUR HouSe maTe

NOT TO HAVE THEM

in your home environment

The cockroach community of a single sewer manhole may grow
to a tremendous number—more than 5,000!

"Oh, no, no keep the lights off! Ah, much better. Now, where do I go? First to the fridge or to the trash?"—What cockroaches would probably say if they could talk.

For nocturnal insects like cockroaches, unexpected bright lights trigger an escape instinct. But not for the Asian cockroach *(Blattella asahinai)*: this unique critter actually runs TOWARD the light!

In the family Cryptocercidae, wood roaches (a.k.a. brown-hooded roaches) have wood sunny side up for breakfast, roasted wood with a garnish of branches for lunch, and pan-seared wood chips for dinner. These wood-eating cockroaches are the only ones to have such a diet. But they are incapable of digesting the trees themselves, relying on the help of bacteria and protozoa to break down the cellulose and allow them to extract nutrients.

Family Tree

A similar digestive system is found in termites, and many scientists believe that both insects are closely related.

If not for bacteria and protozoa, wood roaches and termites would not be able to share their family tree for dinner.

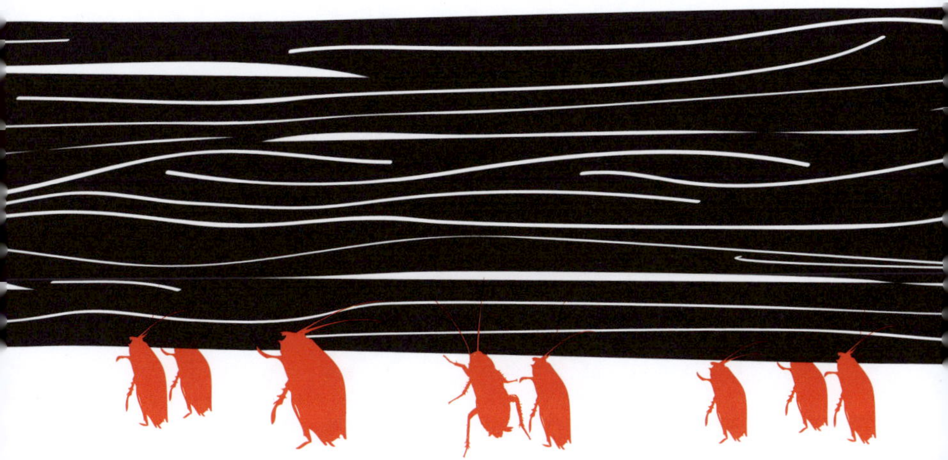

CHAPTER II

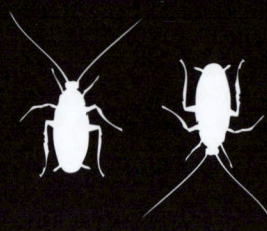

Roach Talents

WHAT A PIECE OF WORK A ROACH IS!

Can the cockroach possibly be the fastest insect?

Let's look at the numbers: the American cockroach can run a distance of fifty times his size in a second. That's about 3 miles per hour (5 km per hour)! For comparison, a man covering a distance fifty times his size per second would be running faster than 186 miles per hour (300 km per hour).

The Australia Day Cockroach Races have been held at the Story Bridge Hotel in Brisbane for over twenty-five years! The event is so popular that over 7,000 people gather every year to bet on their favorite racer. Those who wish to participate can purchase a cockroach for five dollars from the house stables, or you can "breed" your own. For those who can't make it to Brisbane, you can watch the race on television. It is not to be missed.

A roach can turn his body twenty-five times per second—the fastest rate in all the animal kingdom!

Literally before you can blink your eye, a cockroach can run quite far away from you. The vibration sensors in its knees and pressure-sensitive hairs on its legs take only an instant to send a nerve impulse to run.

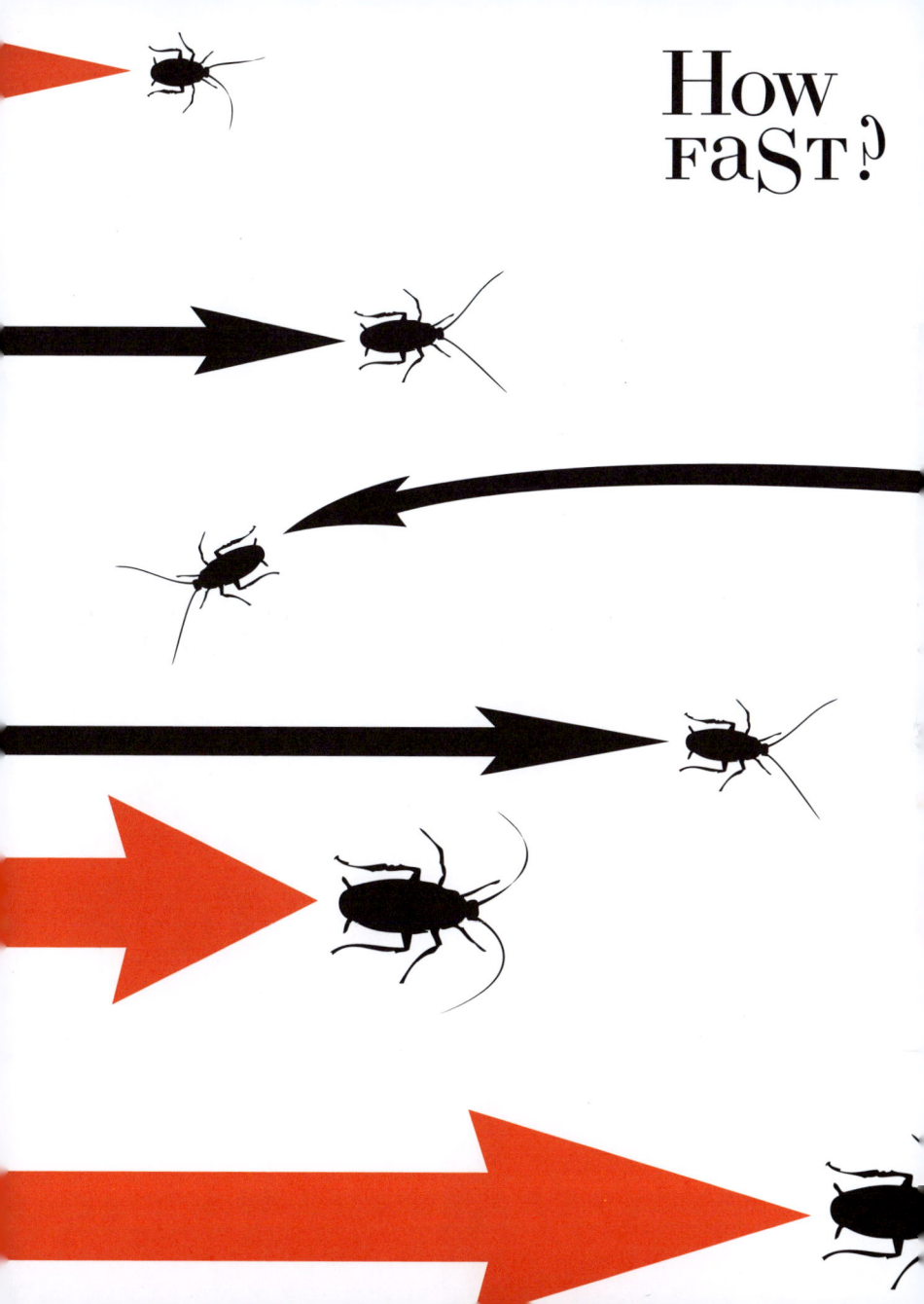

Madonna has said of her career, "I am like a cockroach, you just can't get rid of me."

A cockroach can survive for up to three months without food. With limited food, such as the glue on a postage stamp, he can live for even longer.

Some species can survive up to **45** minutes without air.

Pushing the Limit

They can go one month without water!

One experiment showed that a cockroach lived after being submerged in water for half an hour!

Knowing that the lethal dose of radiation for a cockroach is fifteen times higher than a person, we can say with certainty that they are more likely than us to survive an atomic explosion. That being said, and contrary to common myth, the cockroach doesn't stand a chance in an all-out nuclear holocaust. The real nuclear survivor would likely be the fruit fly, who can withstand up to 68,000 rads of radiation compared to the mere 1,000 rads of our little brown hero.

A COCKROACH CAN LIVE WITHOUT A HEAD FOR ABOUT A MONTH

Why do we need a head?

Well, there are a few reasons that are all quite important—we breathe with our nose and mouth; our brain controls the other organs in our body; blood travels through our arteries and veins to our head.

If we lose our head, we can no longer breathe, so vital oxygen can not get delivered to our muscles; our body is disconnected from its central nervous system so our organs will not operate; our blood will forcefully pump all our blood through the severed arteries.

None of this matters to our mighty hero.

Cockroaches don't breathe through their mouths, they actually breathe through their skin, through openings called spiracles. As opposed to oxygen traveling through their bloodstream, cockroaches have tracheal tubes that deliver oxygen to their tissues.

While a cockroach has a brain, his ganglia exist all throughout his body, and can function independent of the brain.

Cockroaches hearts don't work like ours, they have a tubular thirteen chamber heart. Their clear blood moves under much lower blood pressure, so it is lost at a very slow pace.

The only major problem that a headless cockroach would have is that they wouldn't be able to eat or drink.

In a cool environment the cockroach will survive for at least a month without a meal (and therefor without a head) – that is unless a predator finds and eats him first.

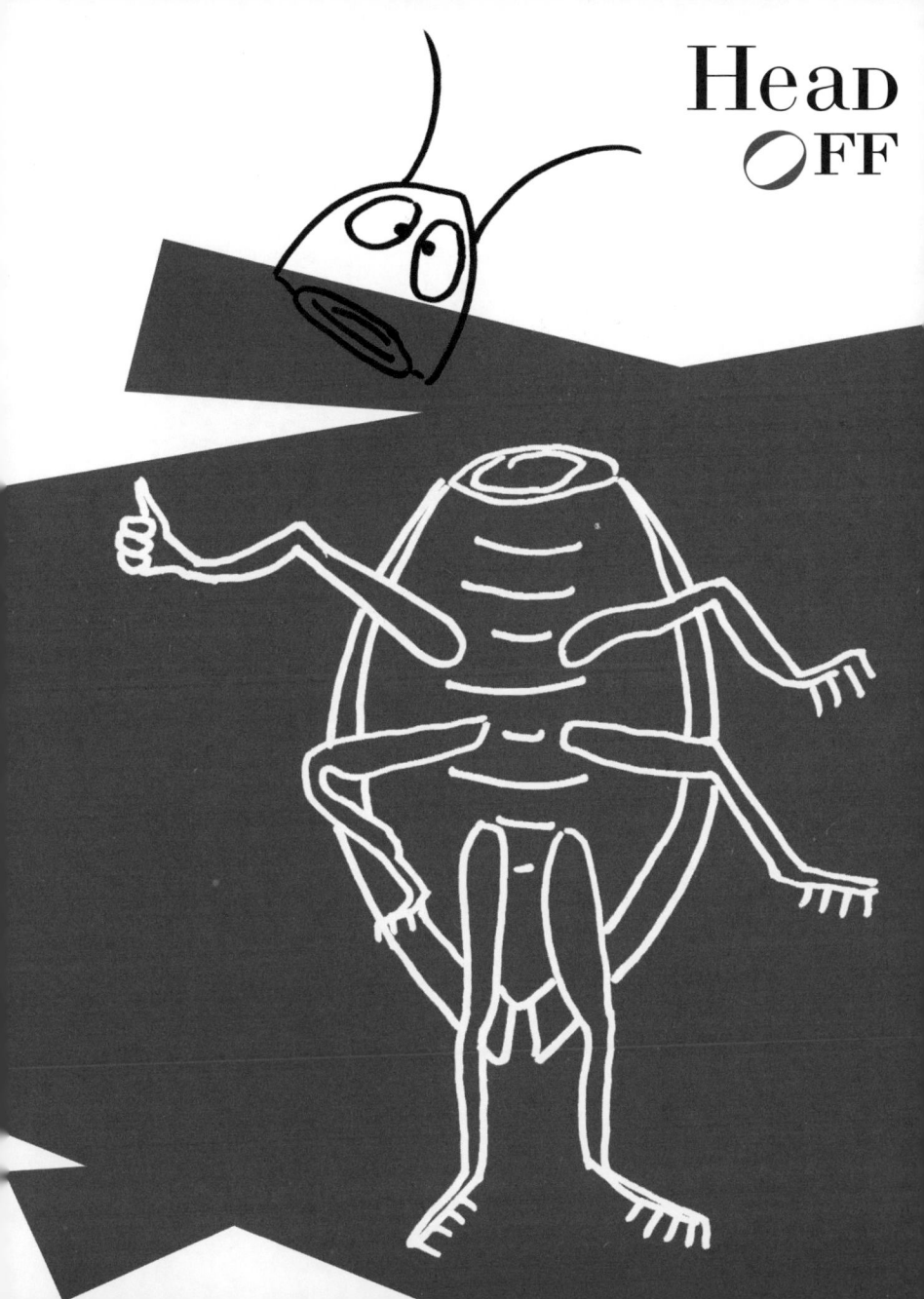

Head
Off

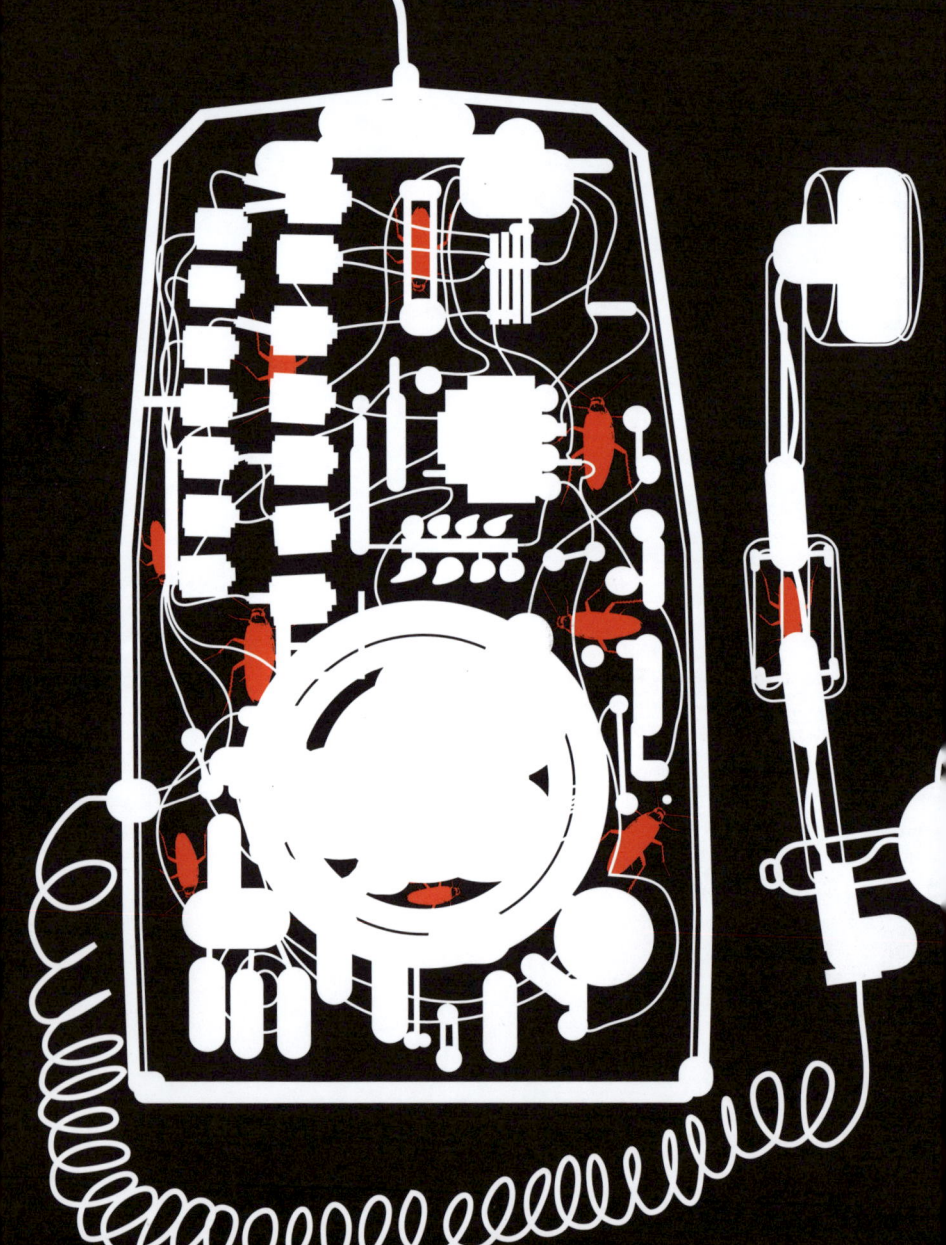

Peek-a-boo

Are you brave enough to look for roaches? Here are some tips on winning the game of roach peek-a-boo:

Look for roaches mainly in the kitchen and bathroom. During the day they sleep, so it's easier to catch them when the sun is out.
Look under the sink and in the moving parts of the dishwasher and refrigerator. Peek into closets, electrical outlets, and other holes in the walls. If you want to be thorough, disassemble the phone, toaster, coffee grinder, clocks, and other household appliances—they love those places too.

CHAPTER III

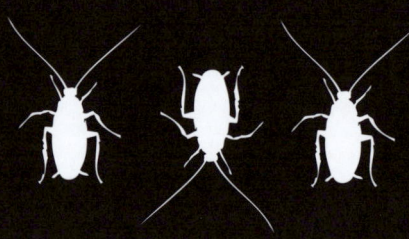

Dining Etiquette

WAITER, THERE'S A BUG IN MY SOUP!

Medicine

Suffering from dropsy? No problem! Cure yourself with a Russian folk recipe of crushed roaches. Bad eyesight? Not for long if you follow the suggestion of many Europeans who suggest boiling, drying, and baking cockroaches in garlic butter. Got an earache? The ancient Roman author Pliny suggests grinding cockroach fat and mixing it with the oil of roses. Allergic to traditional anesthesia? Try an alternative prepared by Australian Aborigines using… wait for it… cockroaches. Indigestion got you down? Ask your doctor if the African American folk remedy of fried cockroaches might be right for you! Is that ulcer acting up? A Jamaican might suggest drinking away your problem with a tonic made of sugar and braised roaches.

If those remedies aren't weird enough, Dr. Kanvee Viwatpanich of the National Institute of Thai Traditional Medicine is studying a salve of heated cockroach droppings to heal sores on newborn babies!

Unfortunately, your doctor will not give you a prescription for drugs made with cockroaches.

For their habit of passively transferring microbes, cockroaches have earned the title of human pests. If they come in contact with food, they can cause salmonella and shigella contaminations. It is believed that German cockroaches can carry some nasty diseases, such as staphylococcus, streptococcus, hepatitis B, and coliform bacteria. If that isn't enough, they're also suspected of spreading dysentery and typhus.

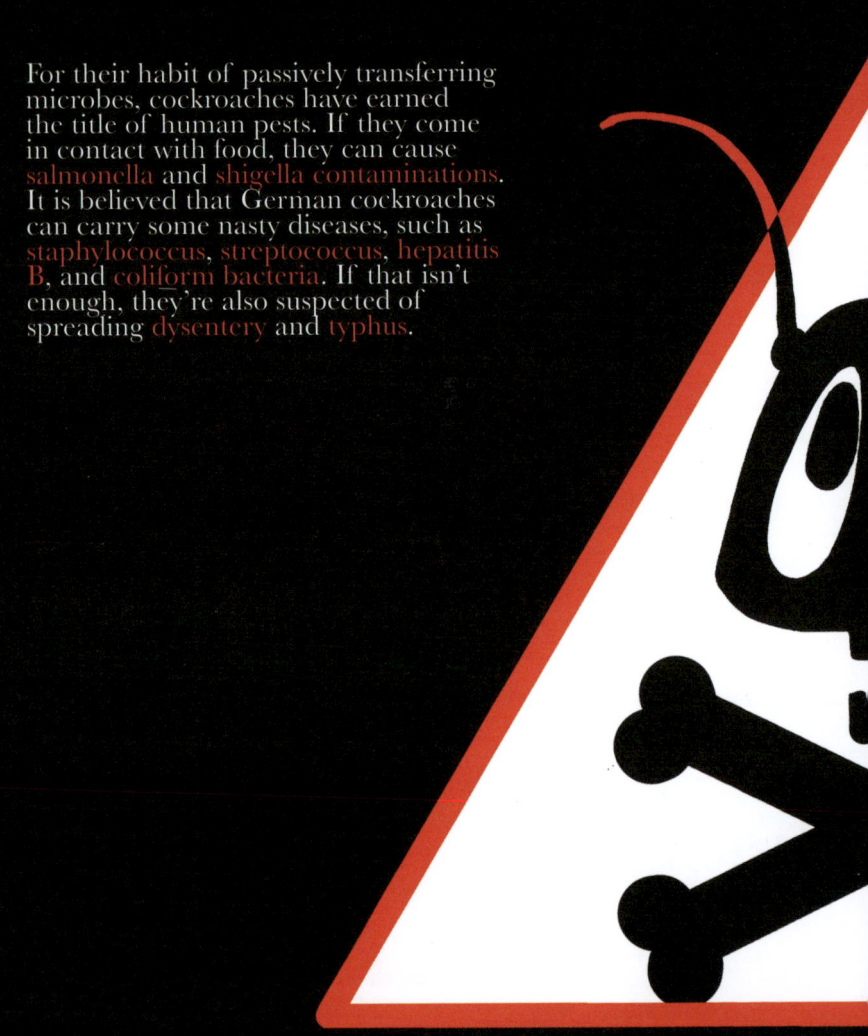

Disease

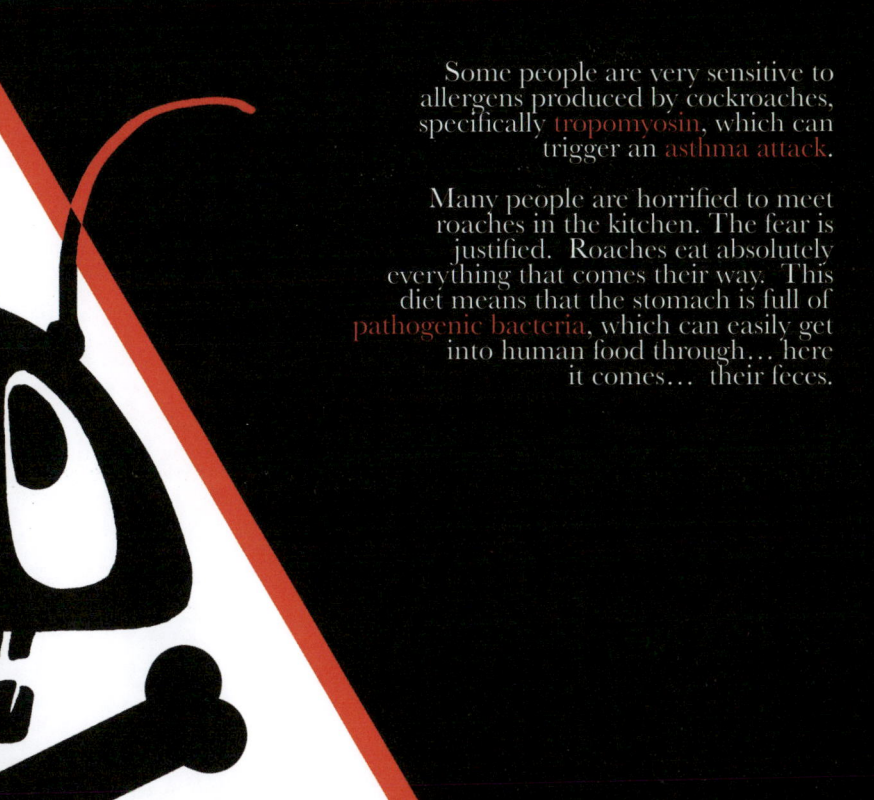

Some people are very sensitive to allergens produced by cockroaches, specifically tropomyosin, which can trigger an asthma attack.

Many people are horrified to meet roaches in the kitchen. The fear is justified. Roaches eat absolutely everything that comes their way. This diet means that the stomach is full of pathogenic bacteria, which can easily get into human food through… here it comes… their feces.

Thai style roach:

A very important ingredient in traditional Thai cooking is the cockroach called Mang Da (technically a waterbug).

This walking delicacy lives in the rice fields of northern Thailand. Mang Da is very rich in vitamins, proteins, calories, and minerals, and its flavor is reminiscent of sweet shrimp. It is a popular dish, eaten whole and fried.

Especially popular is Nam Prik, a sauce, made of steamed and ground Mang Da. For a tasty dish, try sticky rice with Nam Prik.

The harvesting of Mang Da is quite unusual. Late at night, harvesters use lights to attract the bugs and then carefully catch them in a net. "Mang Da" is also slang for a womanizer, so named because of the bug's tendency to fly from one light to another.

Method to prepare a cockroach for human consumption:

Find a fresh cockroach (preferably one that wasn't hanging out in the sewer), then:

1) Remove and discard the wings.
2) Pinch off the head.
3) Pull off the legs.
4) Cut along the middle of the back, being careful to not go all the way through.
5) In a lightly oiled frying pan, on low heat, cook the roach for 2 minutes.
6) Garnish with slices of lemon!

Nam Prik sauce is available on the internet and is reasonably priced. Don't wait! Get yours now, before it sells out!

CHAPTER IV

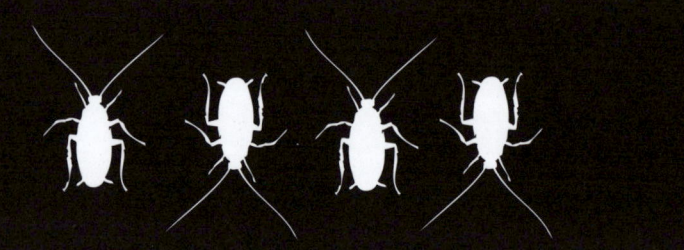

To Be or Not To Be?

AN EXISTENTIAL DRAMA PLAYED OUT DAILY

If you are tired of your neighbor, Mr. Roach, and want him to move out, then listen up:

Stop feeding him.
Do not leave food on the table; keep it in the fridge, in containers. If you are leaving dirty dishes for the night, put them in a sink filled with soapy water. Use a trash can with a sealed lid. Take your trash out often, packed in plastic bags. Don't leave pet food out for the night. Clean the table of crumbs.

Do not give him anything to drink.
Fix your leaky faucets and drains.

Pest Control

Do not invite him to your home.
Cut off all the entrances to your house: put screens on your windows, seal all cracks near windows, doors, and walls. Fill the gaps next to your kitchen pipes with steel wool. Do not store old boxes and papers. Don't leave trash or piles of leaves and branches close to your house.

Place sticky traps around your house to determine the paths along which they travel… Put poison along those paths—you can use less if you target it where you know they live and move the most.

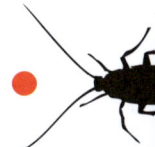

Attention! Follow instructions on the pesticide label. If you have not used a stored pesticide recently, reread the label before use.

Vegas Roach Trap

This do-it-yourself roach trap, which was popularized by a Las Vegas-based TV station, will not only help you catch roaches, but will nurture your inner love of arts and crafts.

Target: American cockroach (possibly German, too)

Materials:
large jar
Vaseline
water
beer or coffee grounds (for bait)
small container (optional)
old sock (optional)

Assembly instructions: Smear Vaseline around the opening of your large jar so the roach cannot climb out. Put the jar down, opening up, and fill it with beer or water, at least an inch deep to insure they drown. Beer will attract them on its own, but if you're using water then place your bait of coffee grounds inside the little container, and float it on the water in the larger jar. The trap is set!

Place the trap wherever the local roach hangout is located. Make sure the trap is either touching a wall or wrapped with the sock so they are able to climb inside. Optional: to make it more attractive for the roaches, put a neon "Vegas" sign on the jar. Let them have their fun for one last time.

CHAPTER V

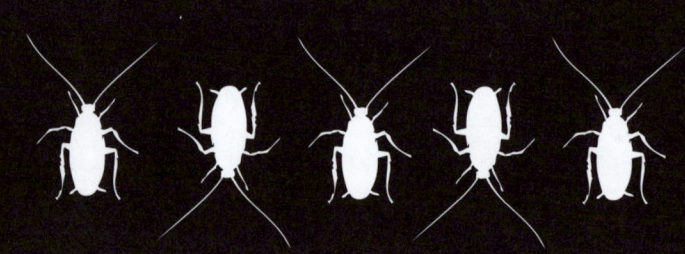

Roach Intelligence

"I THINK THEREFORE I AM."

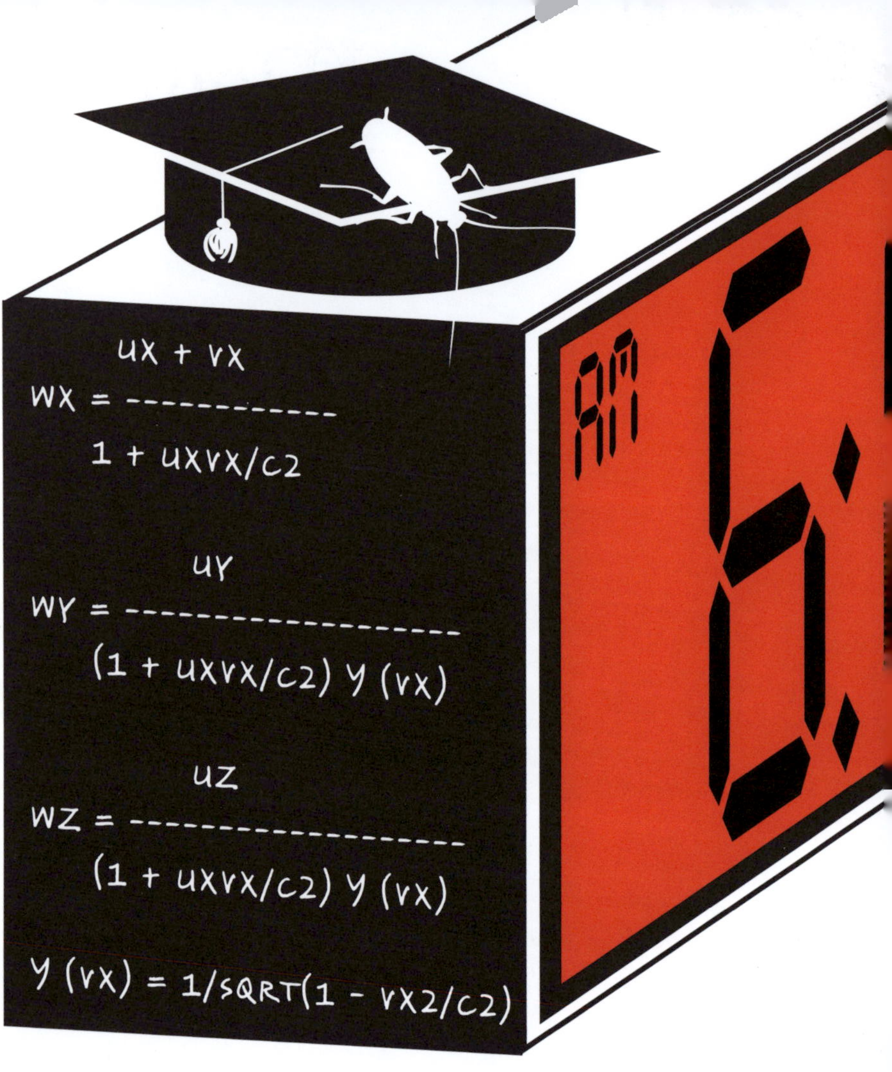
ux + vx
wx = ------------
1 + uxvx/c2
uy
wy = -------------------
(1 + uxvx/c2) y (vx)
uz
wz = -------------------
(1 + uxvx/c2) y (vx)
y (vx) = 1/SQRT(1 - vx2/c2)
AM
6:

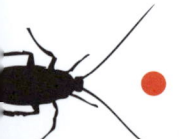

If you are planning to teach arithmetic to your roach pet, do it at night.

Morning Incompetence

"This is the first example of an insect whose ability to learn is controlled by its biological clock."

—Terry L. Page
Professor of Biological Sciences,
Vanderbilt University

Professor Page reached this conclusion after an experiment based on teaching cockroaches to prefer the mint smell (the smell they hate the most) to the smell of vanilla (the smell they love best). Simply adding sugar into the minty water did the trick.

Several hundred laboratory roaches were fed the water at different times of the day. The goal: to understand how long the association memory of roaches lasts.

Roach students from evening and night classes remembered their experience for a few days, while morning students were not able to memorize the lesson and were generally not willing to study anything new at all. Why roaches are such poor pupils in the morning is still a mystery for scientists.

If cockroaches were organized enough to have a society, there is good reason to believe it would be a simple democracy where every roach would have equal rights and decisions would be made by committee. An interesting experiment by Dr. Jose Hallow is trying to prove just that. He placed fifty roaches in a container with three holes, each hole being large enough to fit forty roaches. After the cockroaches assessed the situation, and realized that all the comrades could not

Roach Democracy

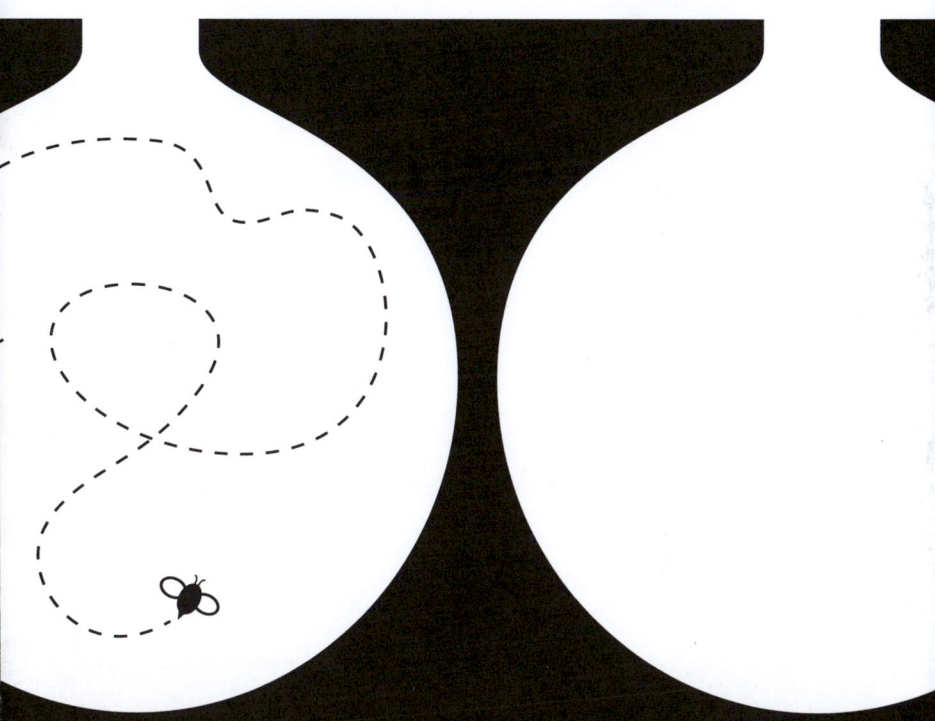

stay together in one hole, the group divided evenly in half! Twenty-five roaches had occupied one hole, the rest went to another hole, and the last hole was left vacant. When the holes were enlarged to fit all fifty roaches, the tiny democrats assembled in a single hole. These results bring hope that if roaches can cooperate to find such a unifying consensus, surely humanity can one day learn to just get along. Truly, a democracy!

Roach Smuggler

A great idea for a prison movie (which you should not steal; it's mine!) comes from the story of an inmate in Texas. With the aid of a trained cockroach, the criminal mastermind ran a racket selling contraband smokes. He would attach a cigarette and a match to the back of his pet and the roach would deliver its cargo from one cell to another.

CHAPTER VI

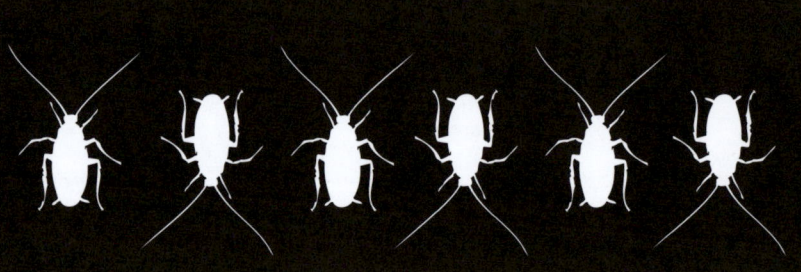

Roach Science Fiction

FROM ASTRONOMY TO ZOMBIES

Relations between the cockroach and the jewel wasp *(Ampulex compressa)* are complex—more like science fiction than biological fact. She begins her attack by stinging the innocent roach on his ganglia nerve, located in the thorax. This paralyzes the roach for a minute or two, giving the wasp time to do some delicate surgery. With incredible precision, the wasp stings the roach in the exact part of the brain that controls his escape reflex. The wasp is now in full control of the zombie roach, dragging him by his antenna into her burrow. If that wasn't enough, next the wasp lays her eggs in the roach's body. When the eggs hatch the wasp babies feed on the roach for eight days and make cocoons inside his body. Four weeks later, the young wasps leave their cocoons. The remaining shell of the roach is left behind, another poor zombie too hapless to survive a cruel world.

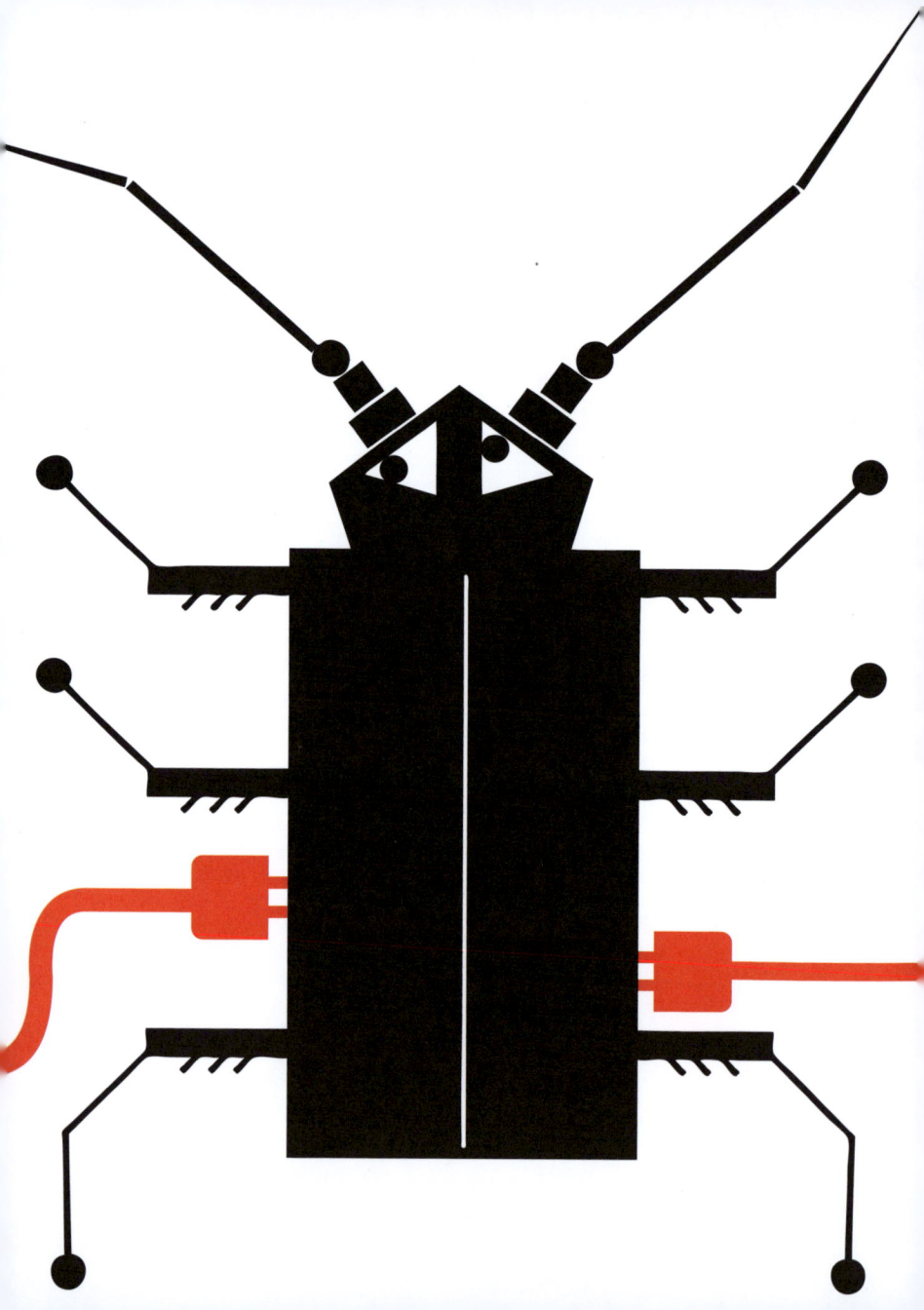

ROBOT 4 ROACH

The Madagascar hissing cockroach (*Gromphadorhina portentosa*), also known as the hissing roach or simply the hisser, is one of the largest species of cockroach, he can reach up to 4 inches (about 10 cm). Surprisingly, he has turned out to be an excellent pilot of a mobile robot.

Created at UC Irvine by Tom Jennings, the three-wheel robot is designed to be operated by a cockroach who is placed on a flexible ball. To keep the roach in place scientists use a simple sticker that is attached to the roach's back. The sticker does not cause any pain to the roach, it's more like his seatbelt. The mechanism could be compared to a regular computer mouse: when the roach turns right—the robot does the same, when the roach goes forward—the robot goes straight.

Even barriers are not a problem for this collaboration between insect and technology. Sensors that are attached to the robot can identify when objects are in the way, which causes a light to turn on in the pilot's cabin. The light causes the roach to run away (instinctively insects try to get into the shadow). Each trip is no longer then twenty minutes. After his heroic adventure, the pilot comes back home to his terrarium to snack on his favorite dog food.

The robot prototype was first exhibited in August 2004.

Per Aspera ad Astra

From the sewers to the stars

In 2007 the first cockroach cosmonaut, named Hope, was sent with Russian cosmonauts to space to give birth. She had thirty-three babies, all of them redheads just like her. The healthy babies showed incredibly fast development and grew quicker then Earth-bred cockroaches. "What is more, we have found out that the creatures… run faster than ordinary cockroaches, and are much more energetic and resilient," said head scientist Dmitry Atyakshin. Perhaps cockroaches are destined to rule the universe after all.

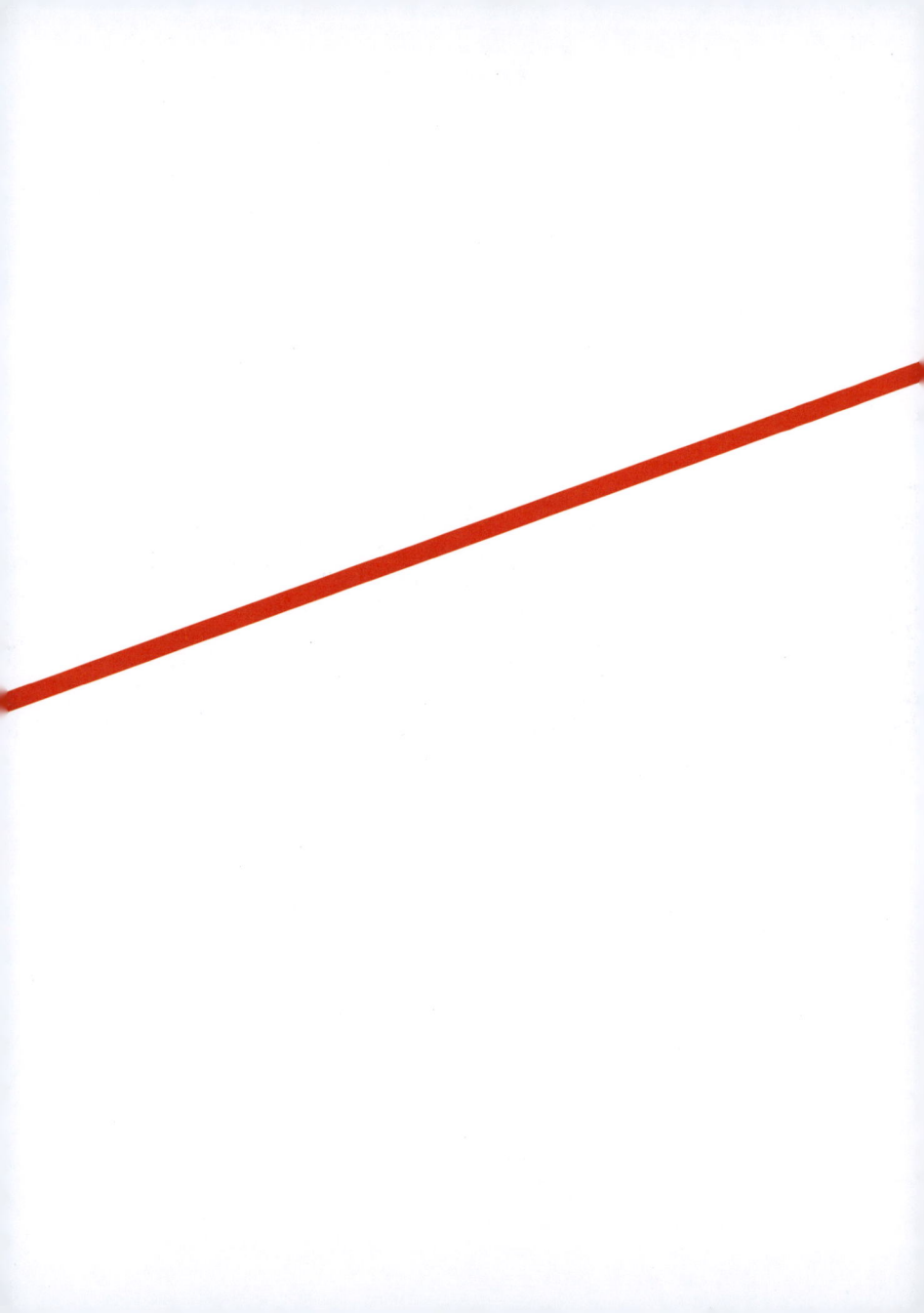

Double Cross

Physical characteristics:
Size: no bigger than a matchbox.
Mode of transportation: four-wheel vehicle.
Smell: cockroach pheromones.
Behavior: roach-like.
External tools: camera, motion sensors.

Goal:
Secret mission to infiltrate a cockroach community.

Method:
Confuse target insects, earn their trust, take over the group, and lead them to undefended positions.

Agent handler:
European scientists.

Project goal:
To study the behavior of cockroaches and evaluate the possibility of using robotic technology for trapping and catching them.

Notes:
Due to the collective nature of roach society, decisions are made in group meetings. Success of the operation depends on getting the robot into the community undetected so it can influence the decision making process.

Future opportunities:
To apply the research data to other types of social animals, such as sheep and chickens.

Success of the project:
Absolute.

CHAPTER VII

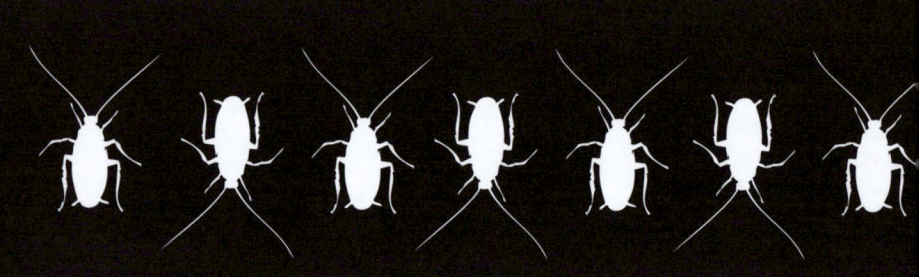

Not The Beetles – The Roaches

LADIES AND GENTLEMEN, THE ROACHES!

In pop culture, cockroaches are often depicted as filthy, disgusting pests. Their shiny, greasy shells make them look like they are creatures born of filth and slime, but in fact they are obsessively clean.

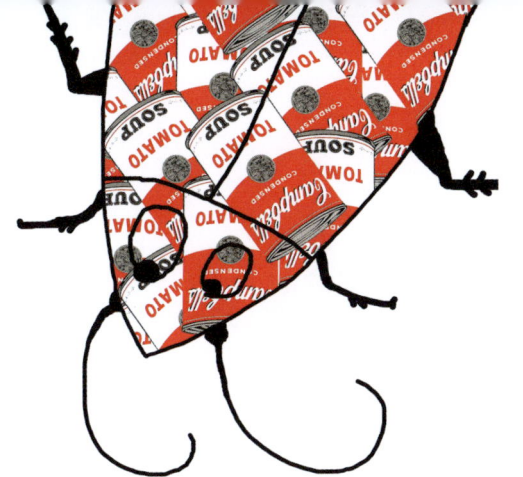

Pop Culture

Dance:
El Baile de la Cucaracha usually takes place at public events in Mexico. A boy wears a loose shirt with a deep-cut neck and a jacket that resembles the long bolero, usually decorated with silver buttons. He wears a sombrero and keeps in his hands a bright multicolored scarf.

Literature:
In Franz Kafka's *The Metamorphosis,* the protagonist Gregor Samsa transforms into a huge, nondescript insect that the book simply refers to as a "monstrous vermin." Kafka's insect is often depicted as a cockroach or a beetle.

The Revolt of the Cockroach People, an autobiographical novel by Oscar Zeta Acosta, tells the story of minorities in American society during the 1960s and '70s, particularly Mexican-Americans. Cockroaches are used as a metaphor for disadvantaged poor heroes.

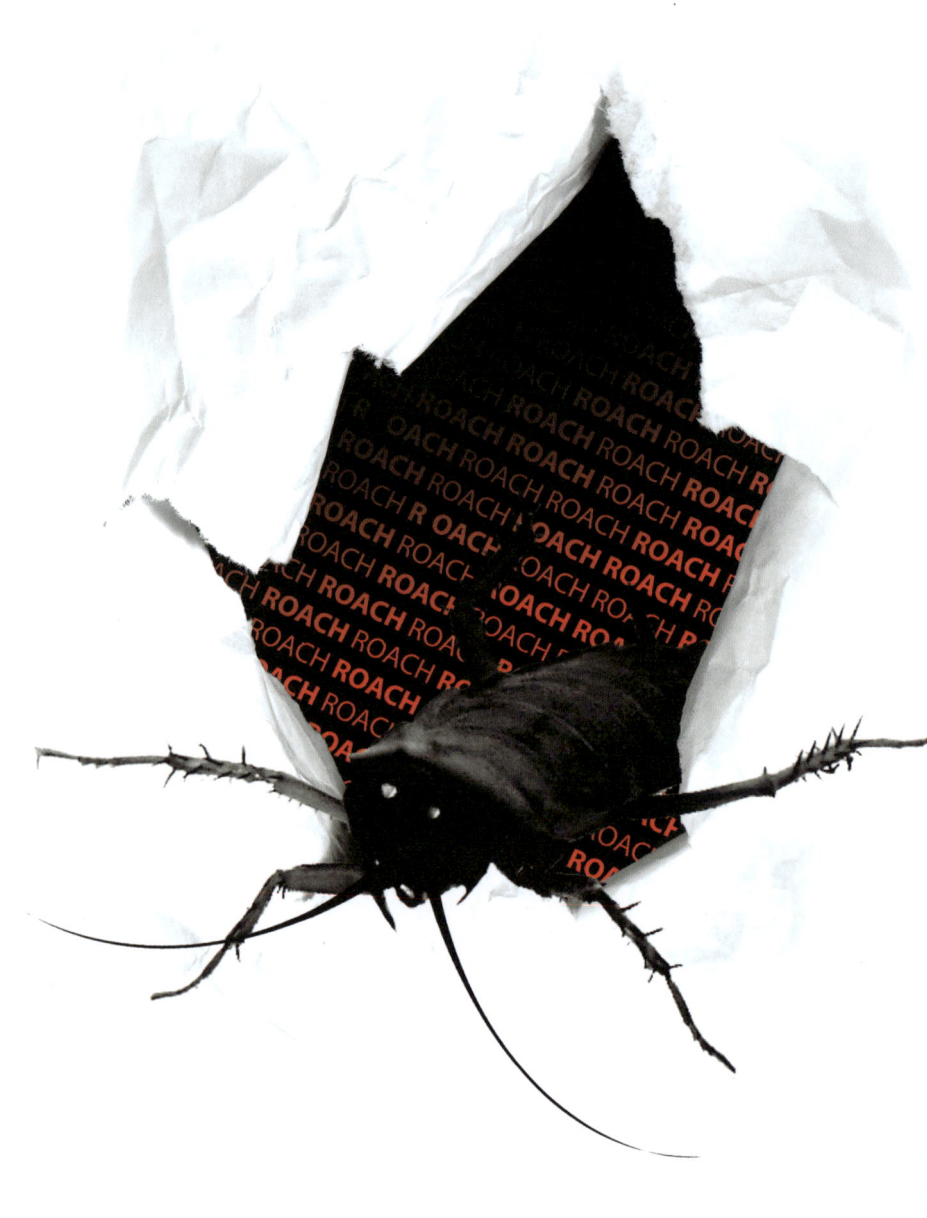

Pop Culture

Cinema:
Twilight of the Cockroaches is a Japanese anime film about cockroaches that live in harmony with a bachelor until his new girlfriend moves in.

In *Joe's Apartment*, many happy and cheerful cockroaches help the eponymous hero discover love.

In *Godzilla vs. Megalon*, a 100-foot tall, lightning-emitting, napalm-exploding cockroach is a rather serious opponent for the giant lizard.

Song:
La Cucaracha—a traditional Spanish folk or "corrido"—became popular in Mexico during the Mexican Revolution.

It goes,
> *La Cucaracha, la Cucaracha*
> *Ya no puede caminar*
> *Porque no tiene, porque le falta*
> *La patita principal.*

Roach Dream Dictionary

After a day of battling cockroaches, if you find no reprieve in sleep, don't fear. You just need to wake up. If you can't shake them from your dreams, perhaps they just want to be understood. Here are some common roach-dream interpretations:

One cockroach means help is forthcoming.

Many roaches means you should expect guests; just don't explain this to your visiting mother-in-law.

If roaches are surrounding you and trying to attack, you may have some problems at work.

If roaches climb on your feet, you better look both ways crossing the street.

Death often greets cockroaches in the form of a bird's beak, a mouse's jaw, a bit of poison laid down by man.

HaPpy enD

Less adventurous cockroaches finish their lives not battling predators, but on their backs. Modern flooring is often too slippery for cockroaches, their ancient legs adapted to walking on leaves, twigs, and other natural and textured surfaces. When a cockroach finds himself lying on his back, he may have difficulty finding a surface to grab hold of to right himself. Unable to flip over, unable to find food, hungry and staring at the ceiling, contemplating the perils of modern life—this is often how the final hours of a cockroach's life are spent.

An Illustrated Guide to Cockroaches
© Ekaterina Smirnova

Without limiting the rights under copyright reserved above, no part of this publication may be used, reproduced, stored, transmitted or copied in any form or by any means (electronic, mechanical, photocopying, or otherwise) without prior written permission, except in the case of short excerpts embodied in critical articles and reviews.

Every effort has been made to trace accurate ownership of copyrighted text and visual materials used in this book. Errors or omissions will be corrected in subsequent editions, provided notification is sent to the publisher.

Library of Congress Control Number:
2010941682

Printed and bound in China through Asia Pacific Offset

10 9 8 7 6 5 4 3 2 1   First edition

All rights reserved

This edition © 2011
Mark Batty Publisher
68 Jay Street, Suite 410
Brooklyn, NY 11201
www.markbattypublisher.com

ISBN: 978-1-9356131-8-3

Distributed outside North America by:

Thames & Hudson Ltd
181A High Holborn
London WC1V 7QX
United Kingdom

Tel: 00 44 20 7845 5000
Fax: 00 44 20 7845 5055

www.thameshudson.co.uk

acknowledgements

My bugs and I would like to thank:

Genevieve Williams, for supporting my idea,

Craig Hymson, who not only introduced me to the publisher, but was a great support throughout this project,

John Zipps, for helping me make english good,

Conor Hunt, for bugging me to get the book done,

my mother, Larisa Petrovna Smirnova, for helping me edit the text in Russian,

Mark Batty Publisher, for believing in this book,

&

my husband, Brian Schmitz, for understanding.

*It was the
only way
I could grow to like*
T̶ʜem!

—EKATERINA SMIRNOVA

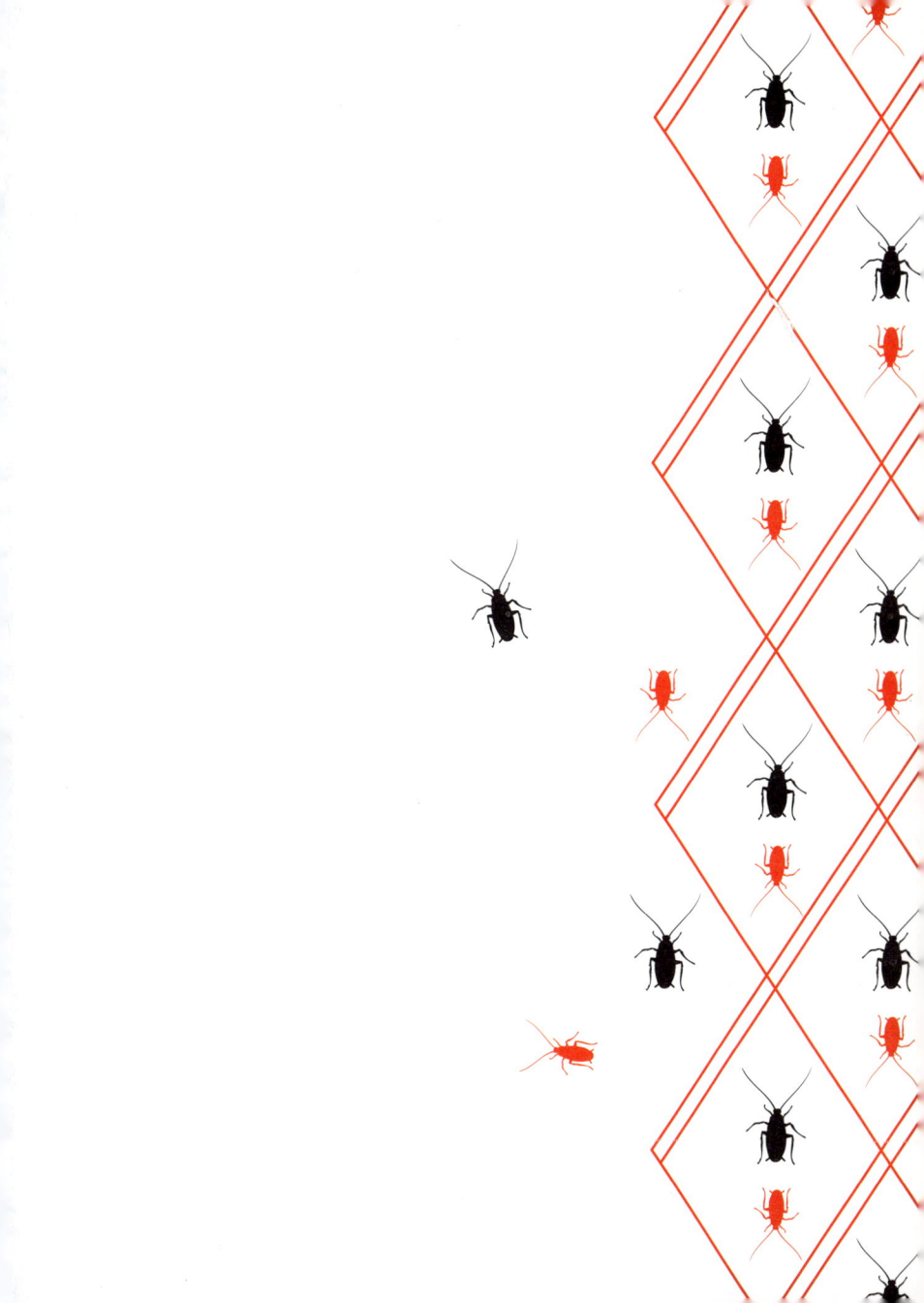